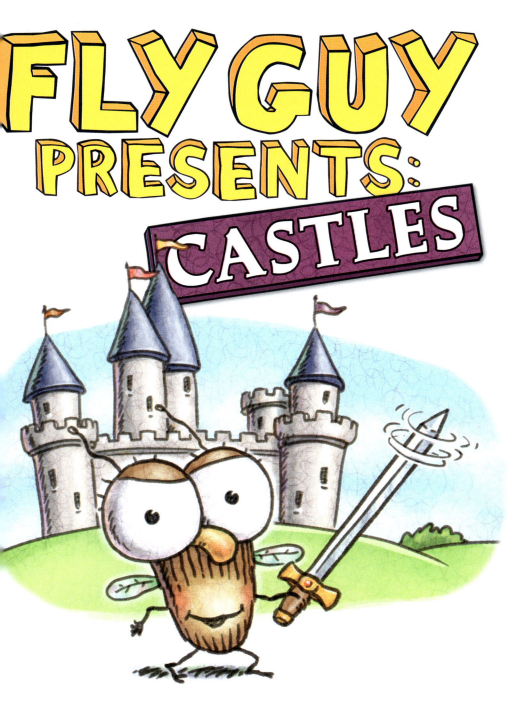

For Prince Kai, Princess Gracie, and Prince Lowell—T.A.

Thank you, Stephen Pow at Central European University and AnnMarie Anderson, for your contributions to this book.

Photo credits:
Photos ©: cover: Alexandre Fagundes De Fagundes/Dreamstime; back cover: Morseicinque/Dreamstime; 4–5: Andrew Ray/LOOP IMAGES/Getty Images; 6 top: age fotostock/Superstock, Inc.; 6 bottom: Patryk Kosmider/Shutterstock, Inc.; 7: Alexei Fateev/Alamy Images; 8 left: GUIZIOU Franck/hemis.fr/Getty Images; 8 right: IR Stone/iStockphoto; 9 left: Denny Rowland/Alamy Images; 9 right: Morseicinque/Dreamstime; 10 top: Carlos Soler Martinez/Dreamstime; 10 bottom: 06photo/iStockphoto; 11 top: VisitBritain/Britain on View/Getty Images; 11 bottom: DEA/G. GNEMMI/Getty Images; 12 top: TamiFreed/Dreamstime; 12 center: Hypermania37/Dreamstime; 12 bottom: Thomas Vieth/Dreamstime; 13 top: Heiko Bennewitz/iStockphoto; 13 center: Heritage Images/Getty Images; 13 bottom: lhervas/Dreamstime; 14 top: Iskren Petrov/Dreamstime; 14 bottom: Geoff Dann/Getty Images; 15 top: mtcurado/iStockphoto; 15 center: North Wind Picture Archives; 15 bottom: Grafvision/Dreamstime; 16 top: Mary Martin/Science Source; 16 bottom: duncan1890/iStockphoto; 17 top: T33385 Abelard (1079–1142) and his Pupil Heloise (1101–63), 1882 (oil on canvas), Leighton, Edmund Blair (1853–1922)/Phillips, The International Fine Art Auctioneers, UK/Photo © Bonhams, London, UK/Bridgeman Art Library; 17 center: Boy with a Falcon and a Leash, c.1665 (oil on canvas), Noordt, Jan or Joan van (fl.1644–75)/© Wallace Collection, London, UK/Bridgeman Art Library; 17 bottom left: Heritage Image Partnership Ltd/Alamy Images; 17 bottom right: Print Collector/Getty Images; 18 top: Prince Edward, the Black Prince, being knighted by his father, King Edward III, English School, (19th century)/Private Collection/© Look and Learn/Bridgeman Art Library; 18 bottom: Tracy King/Dreamstime; 19 knight: Nejron/Dreamstime; 19 sword: Nejron Photo/Shutterstock, Inc.; 20 top left: Garry Platt/Flickr; 20 top right: Alinari/Art Resource, NY; 20 bottom right: eddyo2/iStockphoto; 20 bottom left: Otnaydur/Dreamstime; 21 top: DEA/ S. VANNINI/Getty Images; 21 bottom: Album/Prisma/Newscom; 22 top: StudioCampo/iStockphoto; 22 center: Philippa Banks/Dreamstime; 22 bottom: Culture Club/Getty Images; 23 top left: Linda Steward/iStockphoto; 23 top right: FOTOGRAFIA/iStockphoto; 23 bottom: DEA/G. NIMATALLAH/Getty Images; 24 top left: John Kellerman/Alamy Images; 24 top right: Angelamaria/Dreamstime; 24 bottom: villorejo/iStockphoto; 25 top: Marko Palm/Dreamstime; 25 bottom: Tupungato/Dreamstime; 26 top: Grand Ceremonial Banquet at the French Court in the 14th century, from a 19th century engraving in 'Dictionnaire du Mobilier Francais' by M. Viollet-Leduc, from 'Le Moyen Age et La Renaissance' by Paul Lacroix (1806–84) published 1847 (litho), French School, (19th century)/Private Collection/Ken Welsh/Bridgeman Art Library; 26 bottom: Zsolt Szabo/iStockphoto; 27 top left: digitalgenetics/Thinkstock; 27 top right: ruslan_100/Fotolia; 27 bottom: Dario Lo Presti/Thinkstock; 28 top: Sergey Kelin/Dreamstime; 28 bottom left: Sean Pavone/Dreamstime; 28 bottom right: Daniel Logan/Dreamstime; 29 top right: Anne Rippy/Getty Images; 29 top left: Gynane/Dreamstime; 29 center: Bruce M. Esbin/Getty Images; 29 bottom: Szefei/Dreamstime; 30 top left: bluejayphoto/iStockphoto; 30 top right: Mike D. Tankosich/Dreamstime; 30 bottom: Vlad Limir Berevoianu/Alamy Images; 31 center left: Oleksandr Chuklov/Dreamstime; 31 center right: Lukasz Janyst/Dreamstime; 31 bottom: Kmiragaya/Dreamstime; 31 top: MACIEJ NOSKOWSKI/iStockphoto.

No part of this publication may be reproduced, stored in a retrieval system, or transmitted in any form or by any means, electronic, mechanical, photocopying, recording, or otherwise, without written permission of the publisher. For information regarding permission, write to Scholastic Inc., Attention: Permissions Department, 557 Broadway, New York, NY 10012.

ISBN 978-0-545-91738-4

Copyright © 2017 by Tedd Arnold.

All rights reserved. Published by Scholastic Inc. Publishers since 1920.

SCHOLASTIC and associated logos are trademarks and/or registered trademarks of Scholastic Inc.

The publisher does not have any control over and does not assume any responsibility for author or third-party websites or their content.

20 19 18 17   24 25 26

Printed in the U.S.A.   40
First printing, January 2017
Designed by Marissa Asuncion

A boy had a pet fly named Fly Guy. Fly Guy could say the boy's name —

Buzz and Fly Guy were visiting a castle.

"Whoa!" said Buzz. "This place is amazing."

Fly Guy wondered what it was like to live in a castle.

They headed inside to find out...

Castles are fancy homes.

Castles are fortresses, too. They are designed to keep those inside safe. They have defenses like drawbridges and gates to keep enemies out.

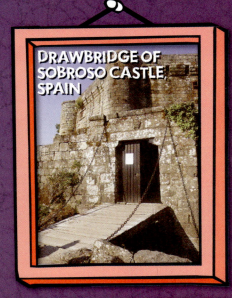

DRAWBRIDGE OF SOBROSO CASTLE, SPAIN

HALTZ!

GATE OF ADARE CASTLE, IRELAND

CASTLE OF ST. MARY RUINS IN LUZ-SAINT-SAUVEUR, FRANCE

People have used forts for protection since ancient times. But the first true castles of Europe were built in the 10th century in France.

That's more than 1,000 years ago!

Most of the castles we admire today were built in Europe during the Middle Ages (around AD 500–1500).

HUZZAH!

TOWER OF LONDON, ENGLAND

CHÂTEAU D'IVRY-LA-BATAILLE, FRANCE

AROUND 950

The first castles are built in France from earth and wood. Wood burns easily, so castles are soon built from stone. Most stone castles have walls that are at least 8 feet thick.

1066

William the Conqueror invades England from France and becomes king. He starts building the Tower of London—a large, square stone fortress.

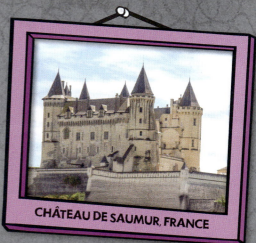
CHÂTEAU DE SAUMUR, FRANCE

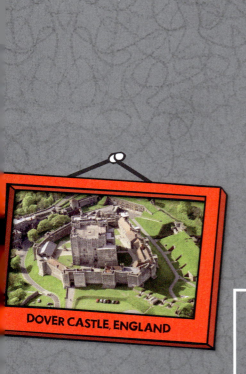
DOVER CASTLE, ENGLAND

1180-1400s

Many castles are built in France. These castles look fancier than English castles. Many have tall, round towers with cone-shaped roofs.

1180

Dover Castle in England is one of the first concentric castles. That means one ring of stone wall is built around another wall.

The Middle Ages are also called the Medieval Period!

If an enemy wanted to take over an area of land, they had to take control of the castle on that land. Every part of a castle's grounds was designed to keep the enemy from getting inside.

PARAPET: A low wall around the top of a tower.

GATEHOUSE: The main entrance.

WATCHTOWER

A lookout point. Guards could see for miles from up here!

KEEP: The castle's main building.

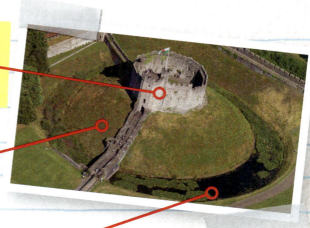

MOTTE: A tall hill.

MOAT: A deep ditch around the castle, often filled with water.

OUTER CURTAIN: The outer wall.

INNER CURTAIN: The inner wall.

Castles were often attacked. So they had many defenses built into their walls.

A drawbridge could be raised to block enemies from entering the castle.

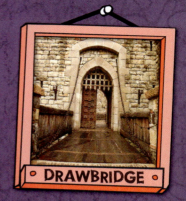
DRAWBRIDGE

PORTCULLIS

A portcullis was a heavy wooden or metal gate. It was lowered to keep enemies out.

Roofs were made of slate or tile to protect the castle from flaming arrows.

TILE ROOF

CRENELS

Crenels were tooth-like gaps in the parapet. Guards could keep an eye out for attackers.

Murder holes were holes in the ceiling. Guards used them to shoot arrows or pour boiling water or hot sand on enemies' heads!

MURDER HOLES

An arrow loop (or arrow slit) was a thin, vertical slit in the castle wall.

ARROW LOOP

Guards could safely shoot arrows at the enemy!

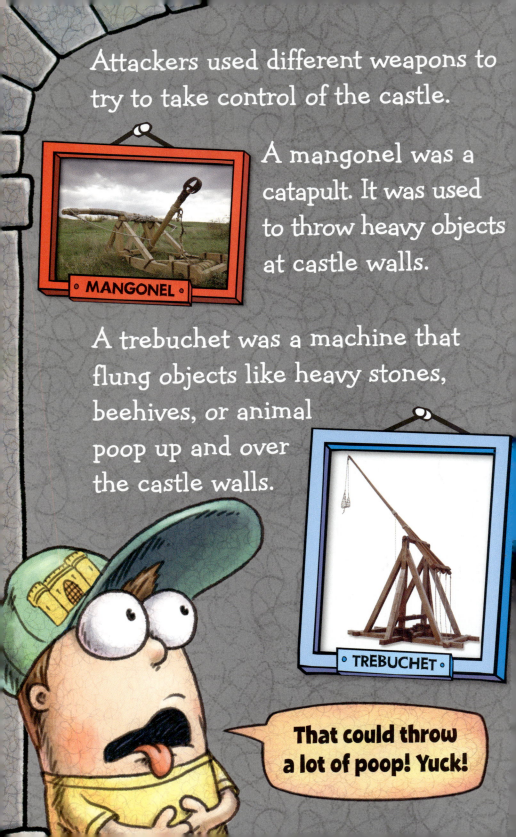

Attackers used different weapons to try to take control of the castle.

A mangonel was a catapult. It was used to throw heavy objects at castle walls.

MANGONEL

A trebuchet was a machine that flung objects like heavy stones, beehives, or animal poop up and over the castle walls.

TREBUCHET

That could throw a lot of poop! Yuck!

A ballista was a cross between a giant bow and a catapult. It was used to launch sharp, heavy darts at targets.

BALLISTA

A battering ram was a hanging tree trunk that attackers slammed into the castle's wooden gates.

BUZZ SAYS POOPZ!

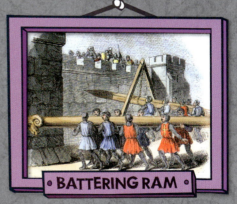
BATTERING RAM

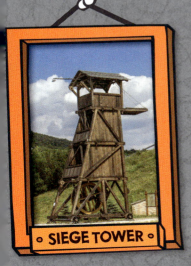
SIEGE TOWER

A siege tower was a tall wooden tower with wheels. Men pushed it close to the castle so they could climb over the wall.

Life inside a castle depended on who you were.

The king and queen ruled over everyone in the country.

There was a lot of land to protect. So the king often gave land to a rich friend, called a lord. As the king's friend, the lord was allowed to build a castle to protect that land.

The lord and lady lived in one of the castle's towers. Their children learned to read and write.

Boys might learn to play an instrument, ride horses, fly hawks, or play chess.

Girls learned to sing, sew, and help run the household.

Knights also lived in the castle. They worked for the ruler to defend the castle. A boy began knight training at age 7. When he turned 21, he became a knight.

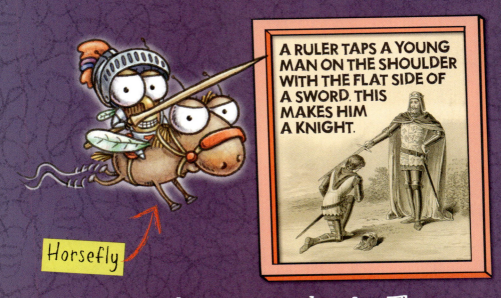

A RULER TAPS A YOUNG MAN ON THE SHOULDER WITH THE FLAT SIDE OF A SWORD. THIS MAKES HIM A KNIGHT.

Horsefly

Knights rode horses into battle. They practiced their skills by jousting. Two knights raced toward each other carrying long wooden poles called lances. Each knight tried to knock the other off his horse first.

JOUSTING

Servants and other workers lived in the castle, too. This included kitchen workers, gardeners, blacksmiths, tailors, priests, doctors, jesters or other entertainers.

KITCHEN WORKER

GARDENER

The blacksmith made horseshoes, tools, nails, and weapons.

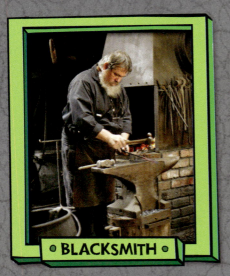
BLACKSMITH

HORSESHOE

TAILOR

The tailor made clothing from wool or silk cloth.

The jester told jokes, played instruments, sang, juggled, and did magic tricks.

JESTER

Many pets lived in castles.

Cats kept rats and mice away.

Falcons or hawks were trained to catch small animals.

Peregrine Falcon

Pigeons sometimes carried messages to other castles!

Dear Parent:
Your child's love of reading starts here!

Every child learns to read in a different way and at his or her own speed. Some go back and forth between reading levels and read favorite books again and again. Others read through each level in order. You can help your young reader improve and become more confident by encouraging his or her own interests and abilities. From books your child reads with you to the first books he or she reads alone, there are I Can Read Books for every stage of reading:

SHARED READING
Basic language, word repetition, and whimsical illustrations, ideal for sharing with your emergent reader

BEGINNING READING
Short sentences, familiar words, and simple concepts for children eager to read on their own

READING WITH HELP
Engaging stories, longer sentences, and language play for developing readers

READING ALONE
Complex plots, challenging vocabulary, and high-interest topics for the independent reader

ADVANCED READING
Short paragraphs, chapters, and exciting themes for the perfect bridge to chapter books

I Can Read Books have introduced children to the joy of reading since 1957. Featuring award-winning authors and illustrators and a fabulous cast of beloved characters, I Can Read Books set the standard for beginning readers.

A lifetime of discovery begins with the magical words **"I Can Read!"**

Visit www.icanread.com for information
on enriching your child's reading experience.

For Terry Stuckey and the children of Chaffee Trail Elementary School, Jacksonville, Florida —S.M.

The author would like to thank Dr. John Durban, National Marine Fisheries Service, NOAA, and David Mizejewski, naturalist, the National Wildlife Federation, for sharing their enthusiasm and expertise.

The National Wildlife Federation and Ranger Rick contributors: Children's Publication Staff and Licensing Staff.

I Can Read Book® is a trademark of HarperCollins Publishers.

Ranger Rick: I Wish I Was an Orca
The National Wildlife Federation.
Copyright © 2017 All rights reserved.
Printed in the U.S.A. No part of this book may be used or reproduced in any manner whatsoever without written permission except in the case of brief quotations embodied in critical articles and reviews. For information address HarperCollins Children's Books, a division of HarperCollins Publishers, 195 Broadway, New York, NY 10007.
www.icanread.com
www.RangerRick.com

Library of Congress Control Number: 2017930903
ISBN 978-0-06-243208-7 (trade bdg.) — ISBN 978-0-06-243207-0 (pbk.)

Typography by Brenda E. Angelilli

21 22 CWM 10 9 8 ❖ First Edition

I Wish I Was an Orca

by Sandra Markle

HARPER
An Imprint of HarperCollinsPublishers

What if you wished you were an orca?

Then you became an orca.

(An orca is an amazing kind of whale!)

Could you eat like an orca?

Sleep like an orca?

Live in an orca family?

And would you want to?

Find out!

Where would you live?

Orcas live in oceans around the world, even in the waters by Antarctica.

Would you like to live in the ocean?

Some orcas feed on only fish.
They usually find enough
to eat close to shore.
Others feed on seals and whales
that travel through the ocean.
Those orcas may feed near shore.
More often their food chase
takes them farther.

What would your family be like?

Orcas live in groups.
Each group is called a pod.
Pods are made up
of several families.
Orcas stay with their pod
their whole lives.

An orca dives as it swims.
It often comes to the surface, because it breathes air.
An orca breathes through a blowhole on top of its head.
Muscles keep the blowhole closed when the orca is underwater.

How would you learn to be an orca?

A younger calf swims alongside its mother. Orca calves learn by copying what the adults do.

A calf learns to poke its head up out of the water. That's called spy-hopping. Orcas spy-hop to see what's above the water.

Young calves practice leaping out of the water.
Leaping helps orcas swim fast.

Older calves play together.
They leap over one another.
They also play
by pushing their tails up
and slapping them down hard.
SPLASH! SPLASH! SPLASH!

How would you talk?

Orcas talk with clicks.

They also whistle and squeak.

Each pod has its own way

of using sounds to talk.

Calves copy their mothers

to learn to talk to their pod.

What if your family had its own special way of talking?

Pods use teamwork to hunt.

Calves join in to learn what to do.

Sometimes orcas use

their clicking sounds to hunt.

Sound waves hit schools of fish

and bounce back as echoes.

That's how orcas hunt in dark waters.

What would you eat?

A calf drinks its mother's milk for the first two years of its life. The rich milk helps the calf grow a layer of fat called blubber. The blubber keeps an orca warm in cold ocean waters.

Orca calves have a full set of teeth when they are born.
Each tooth is long and sharp.
Calves will use these teeth to catch food when they are older.
Orcas share meals.
Food sharing is a big part of being a family.

Where would you sleep?

Orcas sleep in the ocean.

While resting, orcas swim slowly and stay close to each other.

When an orca rests,
only half of its brain goes to sleep.
The other half stays alert
so the whale can swim to the surface
to breathe while it is sleeping.

Would you like to swim while you sleep?

How would growing up change you?

As the calves get older, they grow bigger. Males grow to around 22 feet (6.7 meters) long. Females are usually a little smaller.

Would you like to grow up that fast?

Males also grow a bigger dorsal fin than the females. The dorsal fin is the tall fin on their backs. By age five, the calves help the other orcas in the pod hunt.

Being an orca could be cool for a while.

But would you want to live in the ocean?

Swim while you sleep?

Or eat only meat when you grow up?

Luckily, you don't have to.

You're not an orca.

You're YOU!

Did You Know?

- A newborn orca weighs over 300 pounds (136 kilograms) and can be 8 feet (2.4 meters) long.

- Scientists believe some orcas may be nearly 100 years old.

- Orcas can swim as fast as 28 miles per hour (45 kilometers per hour). But they can only do that for short bursts. Orcas usually swim about 8 miles per hour (12.8 kilometers per hour). That's about twice as fast as people can swim.

- Orcas sometimes work together to make waves that can knock seals off chunks of floating ice.

- Most people call orcas killer whales. But orcas hunt only for food.

Fun Zone

When an orca wants to find things in the ocean it can't see, it makes some clicking sounds.
If the sounds hit something in front of the orca, they bounce back as echoes. By listening to the echoes, an orca can tell how far away something is.

You may not have a way to hear echoes, but you can still get a feel for how sounds help an orca find something in the dark.

Can you zero in on sounds? Get a friend to work with you and follow these steps to find out.

Stand in the middle of an open area and close your eyes. Have your friend stay an arm's length away and circle around you.
Get ready!
Start making clicking noises. Your friend should softly echo those clicks while circling around you. Can you zero in on those echoes to reach out and grab your friend?
Was it easy or hard to do?
Repeat two more times. With practice, did you do better using echoes to find your friend?
Orca calves practice making clicks and listening before they join in pod hunts.

Wild Words

Blowhole: the opening on top of an orca's head through which it breathes

Blubber: the layer of fat under an orca's skin that helps it stay warm in cold water

Calf: a baby orca

Dorsal fin: the fin on top of an orca's back

Spy-hopping: when an orca pokes its head out of the water to look around

Dig Deeper
WANT TO FIND OUT EVEN MORE ABOUT ORCAS?
Check out the Ranger Rick website: www.RangerRick.com
SEARCH: orcas

Photo Credits: Hysazu Photography, Alaska Fisheries Science Center, NOAA Fisheries Service: Thomas Jefferson, Janice Waite, Kim Par Holly Fearnbach and David Ellifrit, Getty Images: Sethakan, Vladsilver, Troutnut, Rasmus-Raahauge, Jeff Foott, Rebecca-Belleni-Photogra

Dogs such as beagles were used to hunt rabbits.

Horses were used for travel, battles, hunts, and farmwork.

FLIES LIVED IN CASTLES, TOO!

Most parts of a castle were crowded, shared spaces.

Only the ruling family had its own rooms. These rooms smelled good because fresh herbs hung from the walls.

• LANGEAIS CASTLE, FRANCE •

• FRESH HERBS •

The castle toilet was called a garderobe. It was a wooden or stone slab with a hole in the middle. Waste fell down a chute. No one liked shoveling it out, but someone had to do it! This person was called the gong farmer.

• GARDEROBE •

The dungeon was often at the very bottom of the castle, below the basement. Some dungeons were rooms in high towers. Prisoners were held here.

The only way in or out was through a trapdoor in the floor.

Celebrations were held in the castle's main room—the great hall.

Fish from fish ponds or the moat might be served at a feast, along with beef and lamb. Wild birds would be baked into pies.

YUMZZIE!

Desserts included custards and fruit tarts. They were usually sweetened with honey.

FRUIT TART

HONEY

Food was eaten off plates made of wood or pottery. They were called trenchers. Sometimes stale pieces of bread were used as trenchers. Everyone had a spoon and knife, but there were no forks.

Who needs forks?!

TRENCHERS

There are castles—and buildings like castles—all around the world. Many of them were built after the Middle Ages.

The Kremlin in Russia has five palaces and four cathedrals.

Himeji Castle in Japan is known as "White Egret Castle." It looks like a beautiful bird!

Great Egret

Alcázar de Segovia in Spain looks like the bow of a ship.

Château de Villandry in France is famous for its gardens.

Lal Qila (or Red Fort) in India is named for its red sandstone walls.

CASTLEZ EVERYWHERE!

Castles have inspired the work of many artists and authors.

Neuschwanstein Castle in Germany inspired artist Walt Disney to build Sleeping Beauty Castle at Disneyland Park.

NEUSCHWANSTEIN CASTLE

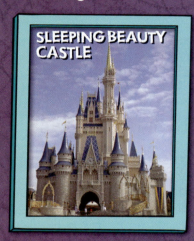

SLEEPING BEAUTY CASTLE

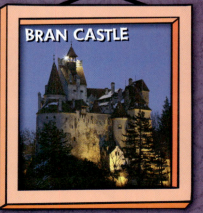

BRAN CASTLE

Bran Castle in Romania is also called Dracula's Castle. Bram Stoker wrote *Dracula* in 1897. Many people believe this castle was his inspiration.

Castles today are often museums. Some are still home to modern families.

Prague Castle is the home of the Czech president.

Windsor Castle is the oldest castle in the world to still have people living in it.

At Blarney Castle, visitors kiss the Blarney Stone.

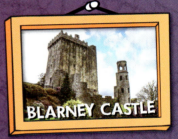

There's even a castle in New York City!

Belvedere Castle is actually a weather station.

"It was fun to learn about castles," Buzz told Fly Guy. "It's even more fun to make our own!"

Buzz and Fly Guy could not wait for their next field trip.